Rosie is daring. Verna is tough.
Girls on the loose in wild garb who can't shake
each other's company.

Story and Illustrations by Jamie Wainright

Copyright © Wainright & Associates, 2011. www.darlenesisters.com
Published by White River Press, Amherst, Mass. www.whiteriverpress.com
All rights reserved. ISBN: 978-935052-59-3

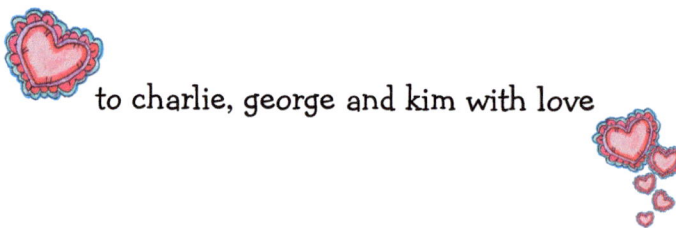

to charlie, george and kim with love

The darlene sisters, Rosie and Verna.
Girls on the loose in wild garb who can't shake each other's company.

They don't want you to ask about Earl; he is just an average guy who annoys them. Earl is the third wheel who always acts like a flat tire.

And then there is Emma, who has them all wrapped around her little paw!

Rosie is a daring woman who is always pushing the limits. She speaks her mind, which can sometimes get her in trouble, but she is always a true friend to those closest to her. Her wild spirit is what makes Rosie so endearing to her friends.

Rosie

R

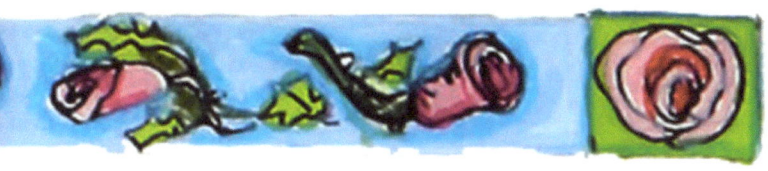

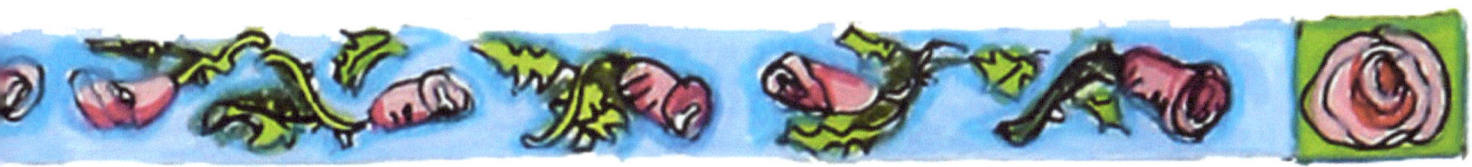

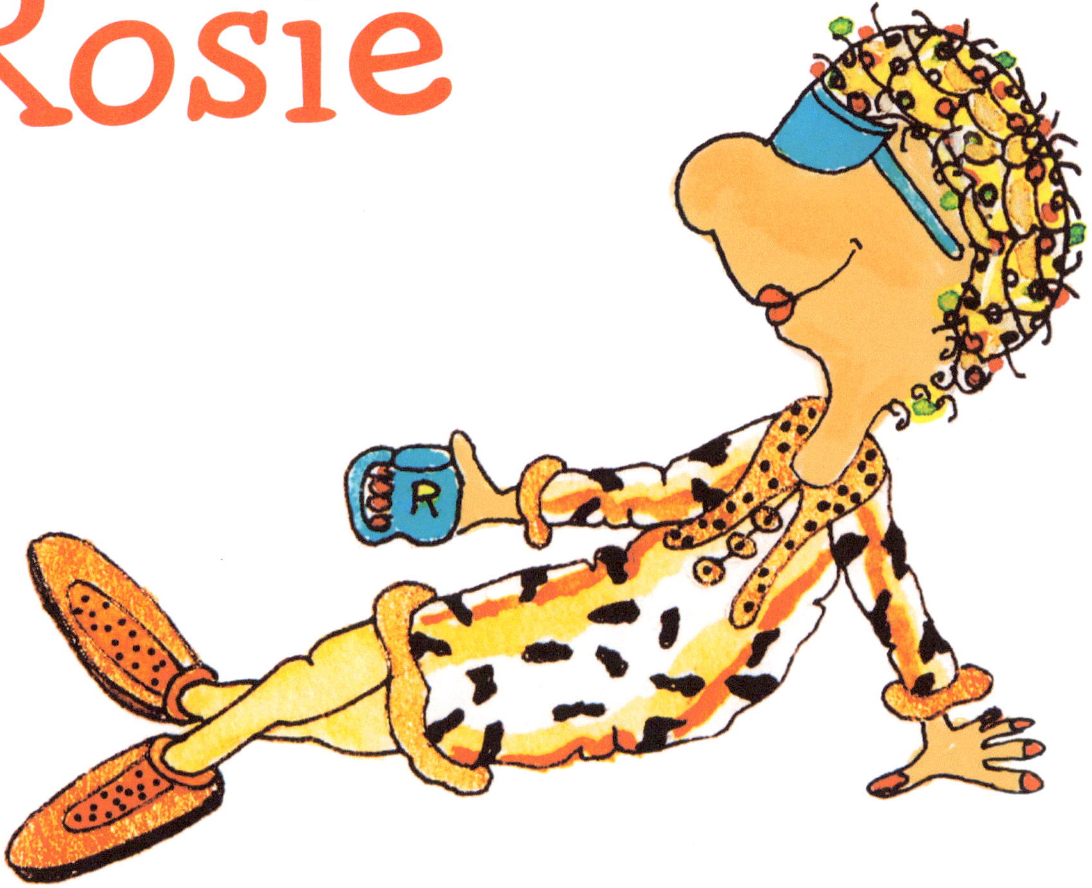

Verna

V

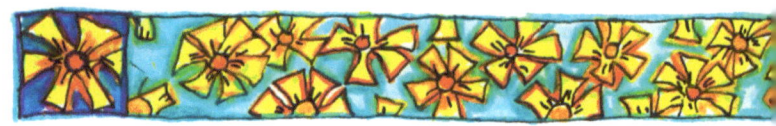

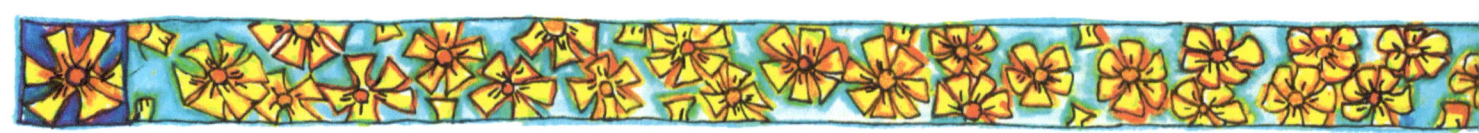

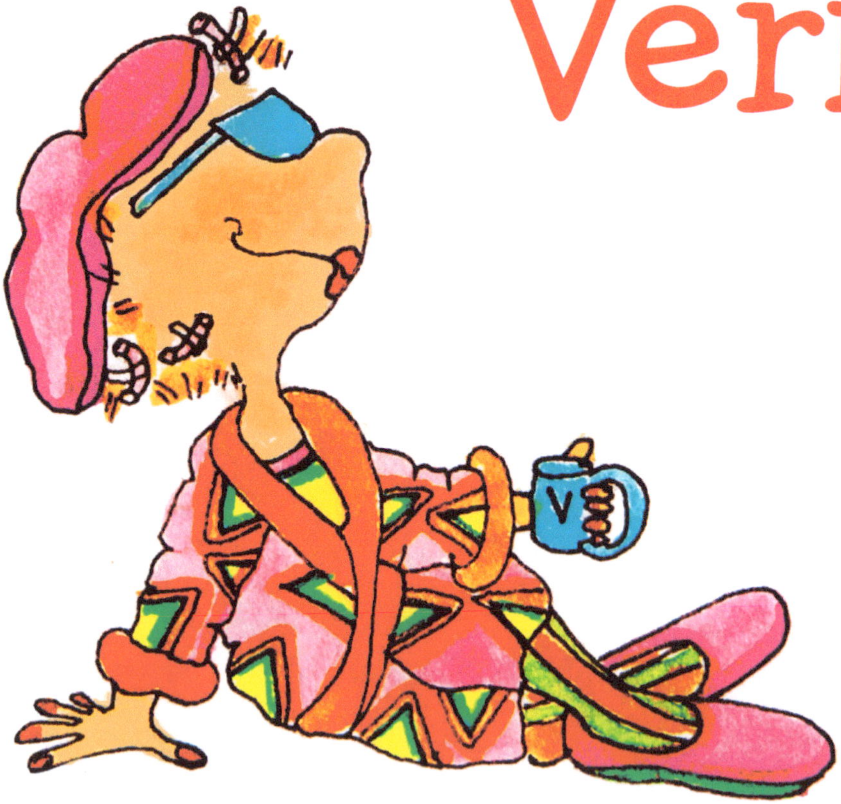

Verna is tough but toes the line. She tries to keep the gang out of trouble, but is often the one who finds it. A dependable woman who always has her heart in the right place.

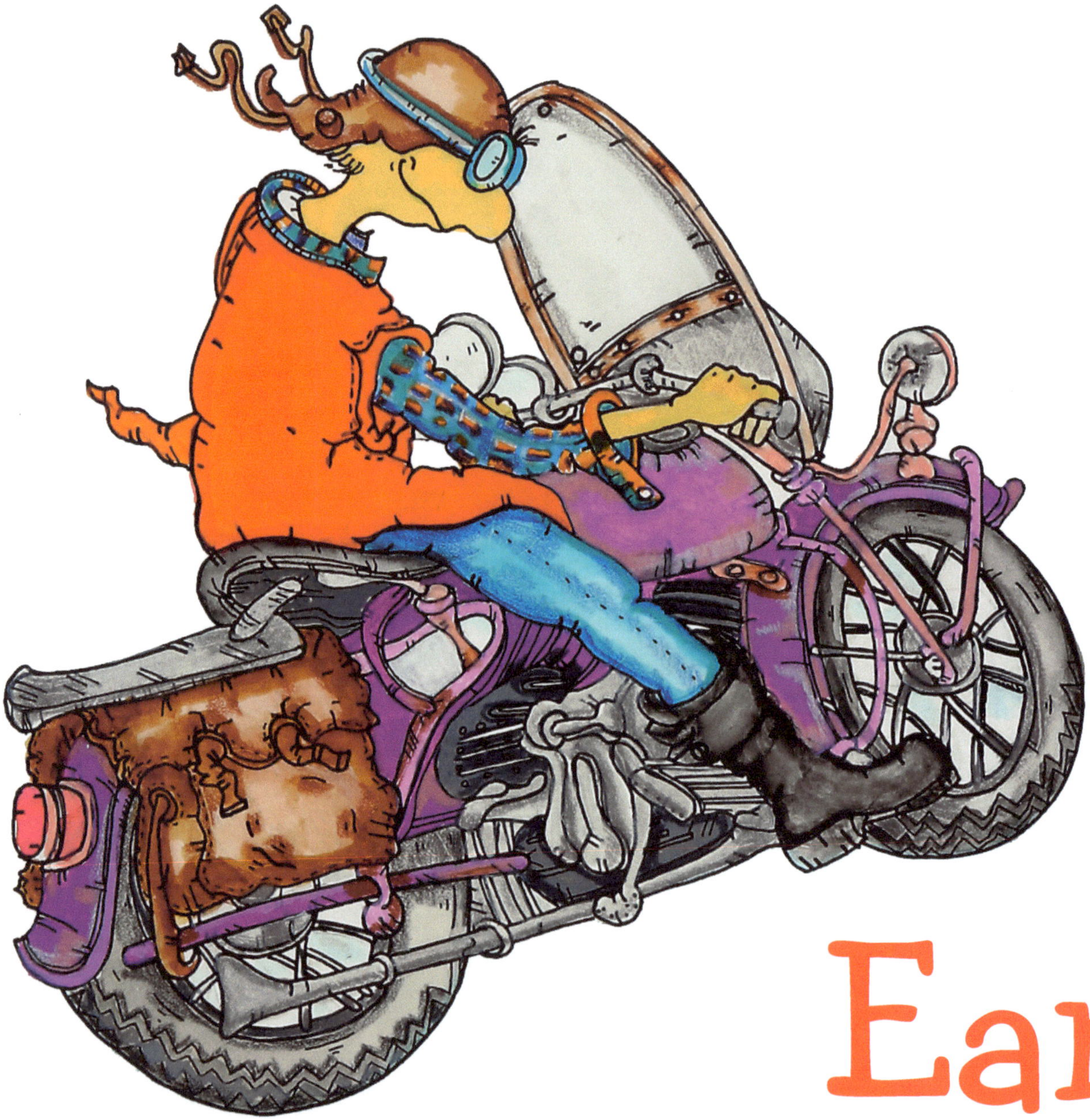

Earl

The average guy next door, Earl knows everything about nothing and nothing about everything. He is always watching out for the girls, even when they don't want him to. And in the end they all watch out for each other.

Emma has the girls and Earl well trained. She knows the first sandwich is hers, and makes sure to be the last one off the couch. Emma always gets what she wants, but gives loads of love and support in return!

Emma

Rosie & Verna:
Having an off balance day.

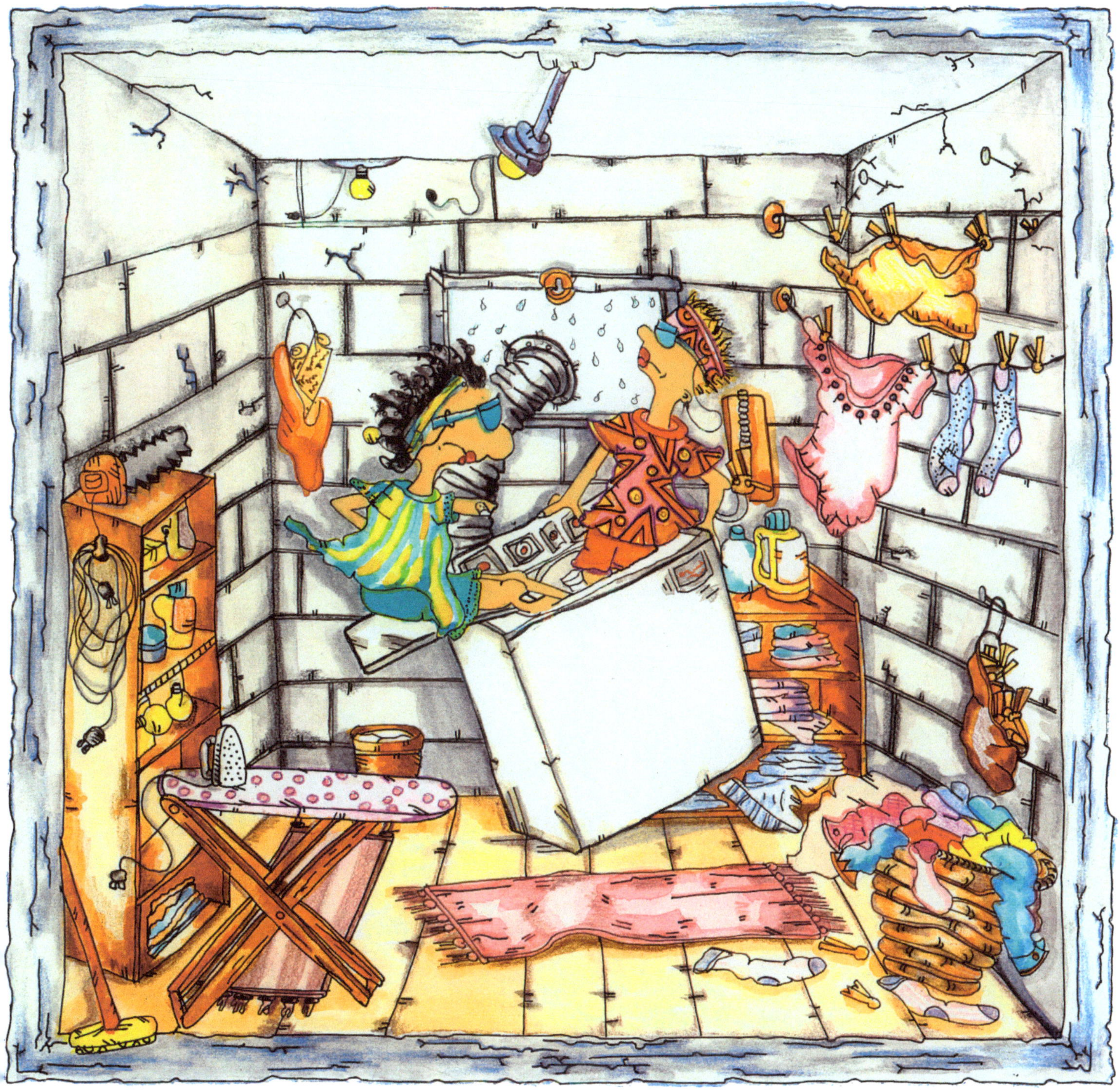

The Girls & Earl:
Discuss the issue of short term memory.

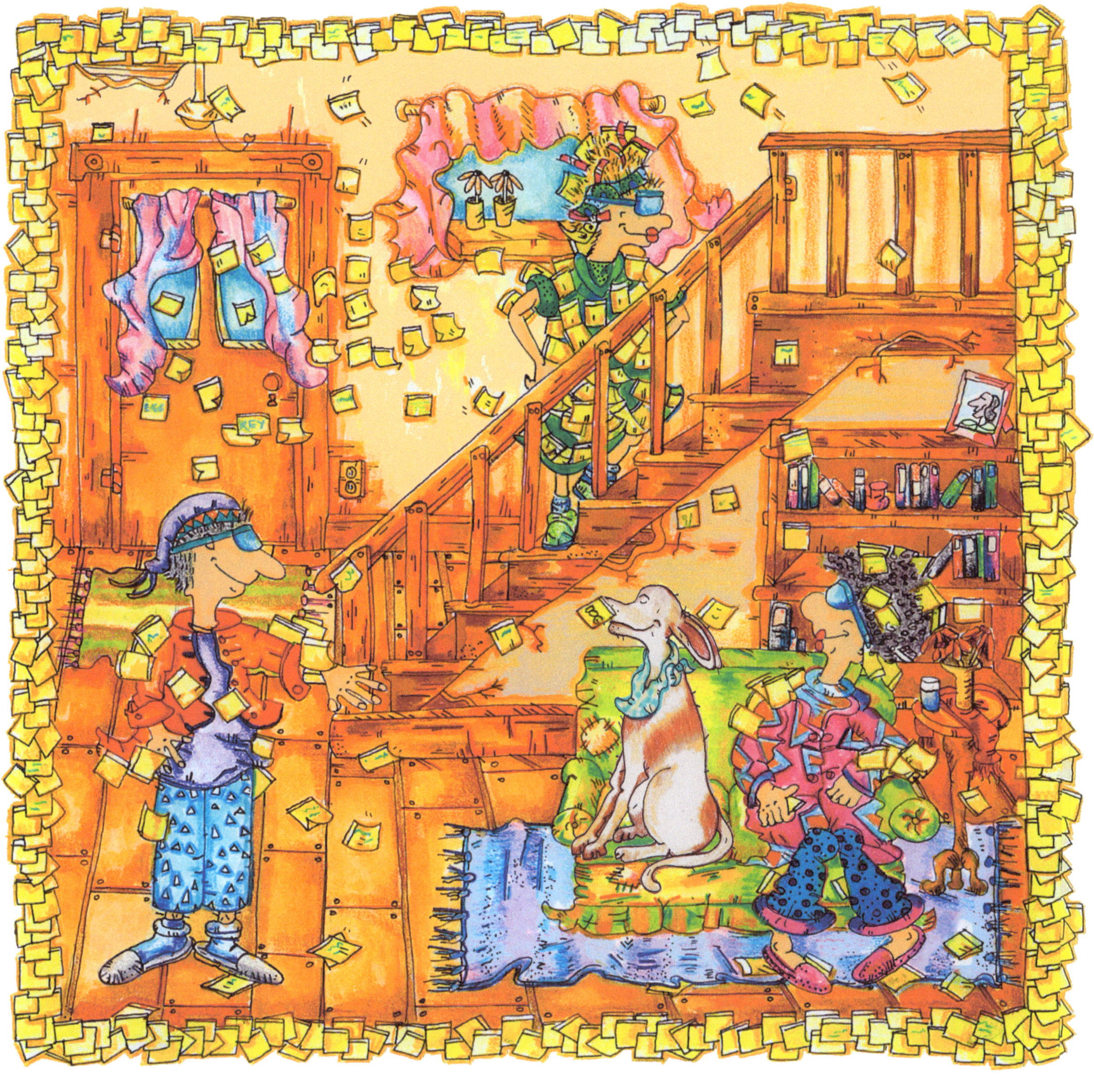
KEY

The Girls & Earl:
Are optimistic about working off
two muffin tops and a watermelon waist.

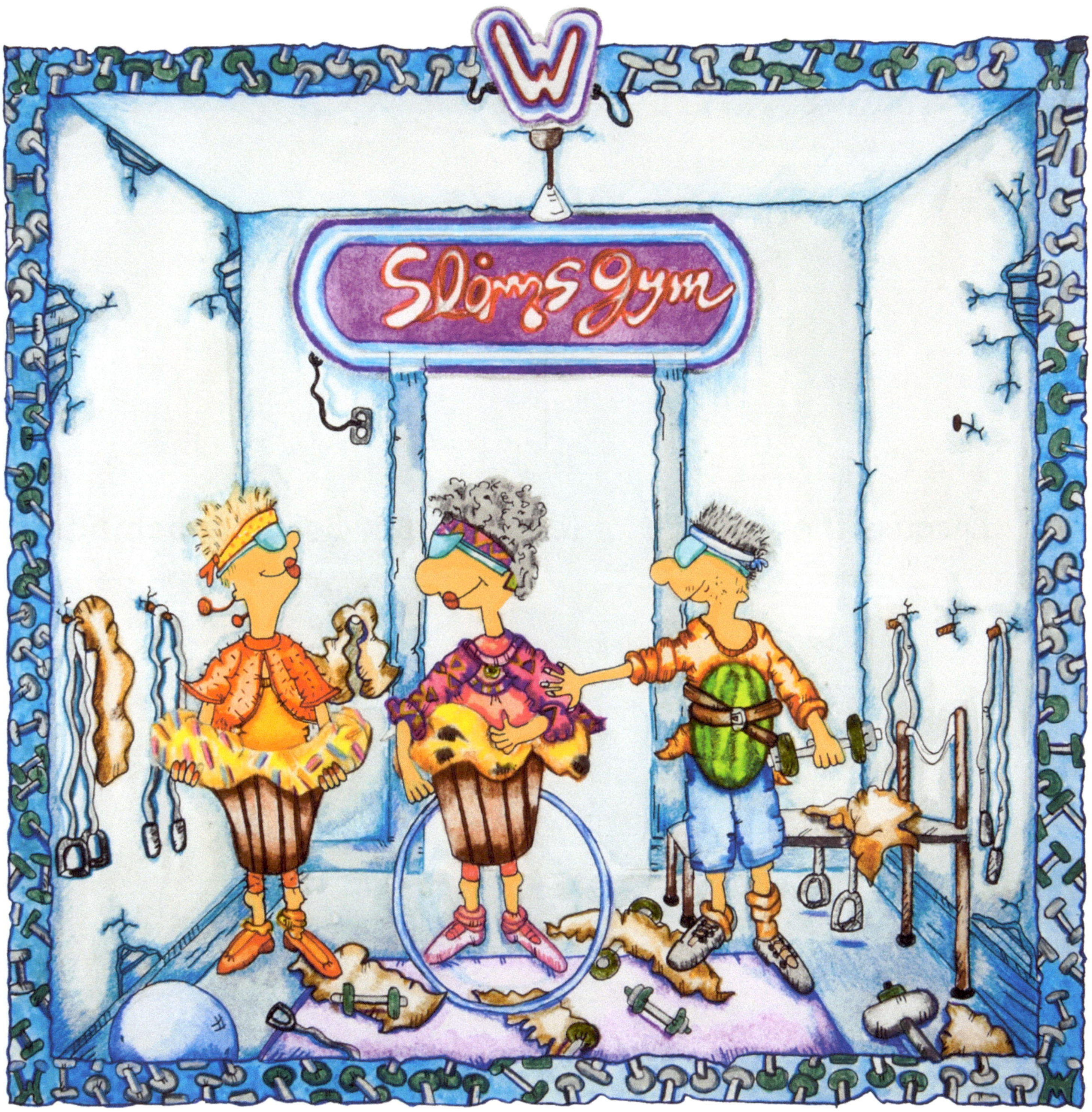

Slims gym

The Girls & Earl:
Discuss the benefits of leaving their baggage behind.

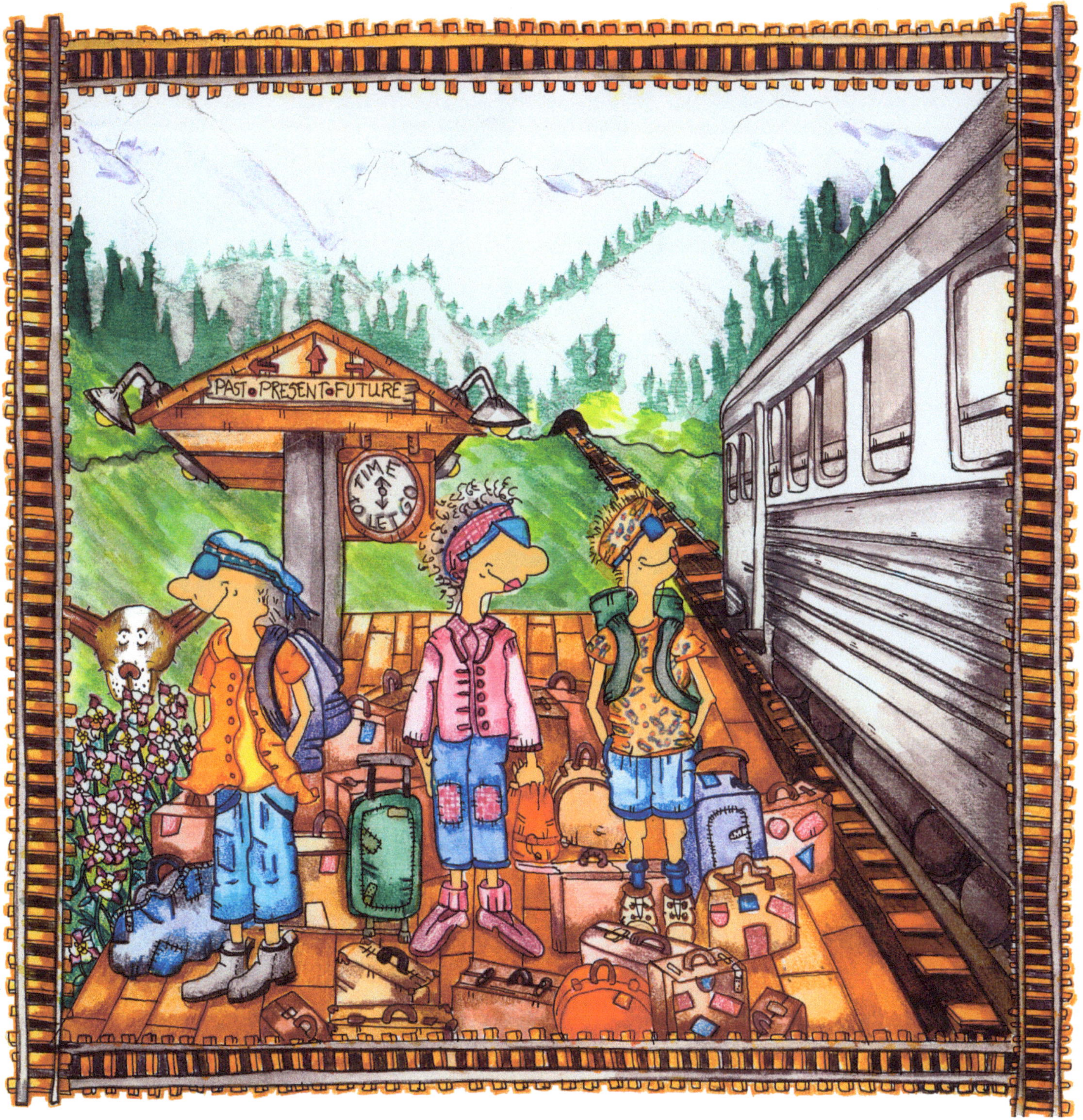
PAST • PRESENT • FUTURE
TIME TO LET GO

Rosie & Verna agree:
The best decisions are made here.

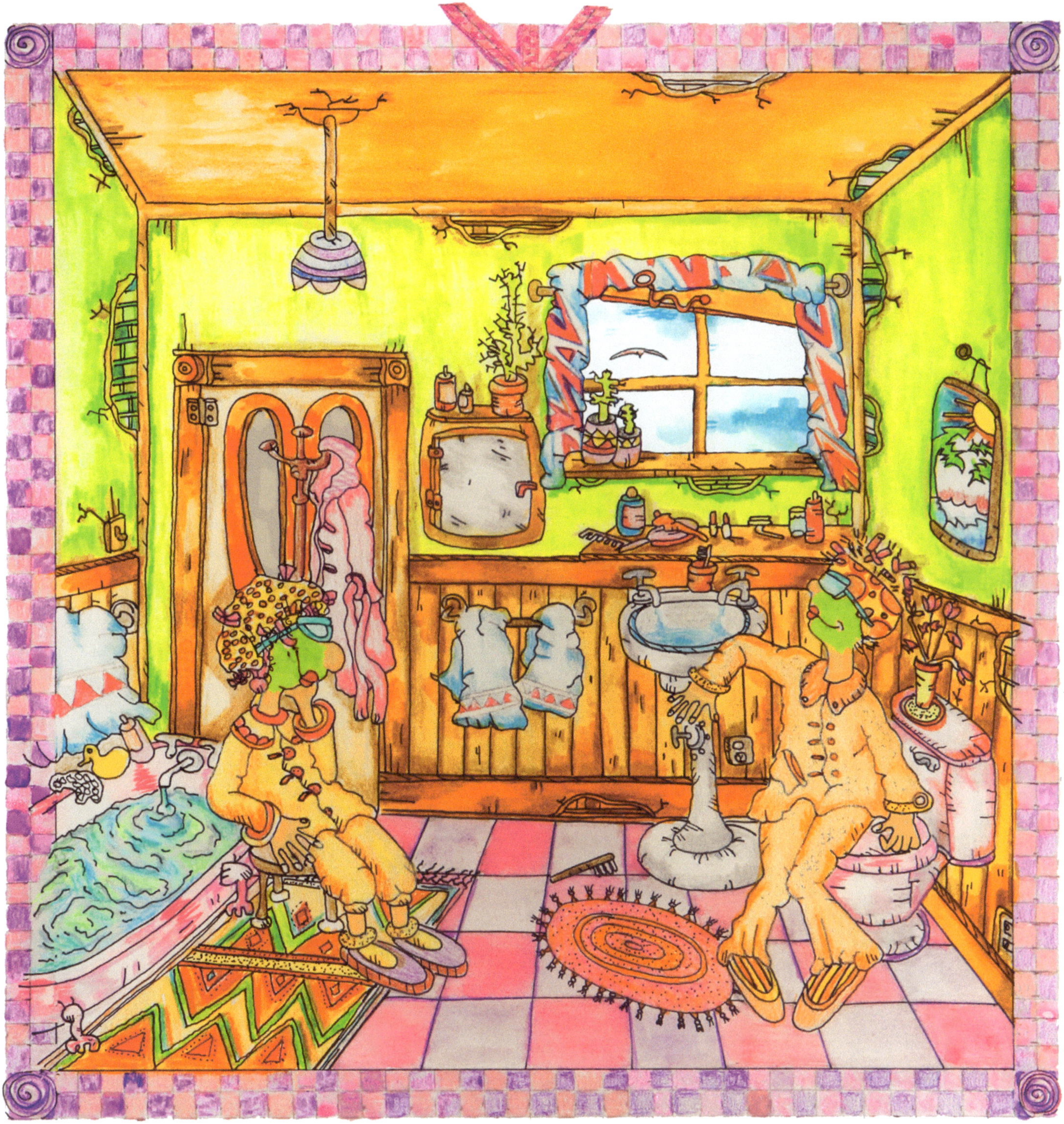

The darlene sisters and Earl have been a part of my life for as long as I can remember. They represent voices inside all of us, and live out in illustration our everyday situations, observations of life, and day-to-day happenings.

Rosie and Verna are characters born of my mother, Caroline and her best friend, Louise ("Wee-zee"). Mother and Louise went everywhere together. As a young girl, I would listen to their conversations while riding in the back seat of the car, hearing from them about the everyday happenings that are a part of us all. When it came to naming their personas, I wanted old-fashioned names that seemed to fit together like peanut butter and jelly and, like them, would stand the test of time. I invented Earl as the person who we all know that just hangs around. Young or old, there is an Earl for all of us.

Humor is a big part of my family. Noticing the smallest event that someone else might miss, our family made a story of it. As a girl, I drew the darlene sisters all the time on the margins of my homework or in the basement "art studio" my father set up for me. I portray these characters as being timeless, and have used them to make cards for family and friends throughout my life.

I have always had an interest in pursuing the voices of the darlene sisters' and Earl's life happenings using my feelings, experiences, and view of the world. As I grow older, my life's ventures, trials, and family happenings expand these characters. Earl's clothing will sometimes stem from my two sons, Charlie and George, and their favorite outfits as they were growing up. Many of the newer pieces have also begun to include our pet dog, Emma. Whether in the grocery store, traveling, home, or at work, I am taking notes for the voices and humor of the darlene sisters and Earl as we cross paths in all I do, everywhere, everyday.

I have a traditional training in art with undergraduate and graduate school degrees. Both of my parents supported and encouraged my art career, especially my father who was a great lover of watercolor works. A successful career in fine arts and graphic design led to my current position as full-time Professor and Chairperson of the Art Department at Westfield State University in Westfield, Massachusetts.

~jamie wainright

www.ingramcontent.com/pod-product-compliance
Lightning Source LLC
Chambersburg PA
CBHW042303060426
42446CB00039B/213
9781935052593